Disney
Songs of the 2010s

SOPRANO OR BELTER

All accompaniments performed by Brendan Fox.

To access recorded accompaniments online, visit:
www.halleonard.com/mylibrary

"Enter Code"
3522-4121-3971-2168

ISBN 978-1-5400-9665-4

Characters and Artwork © Disney
Disney/Pixar elements © Disney/Pixar

Visit Hal Leonard Online at
www.halleonard.com

Contact us:
Hal Leonard
7777 West Bluemound Road
Milwaukee, WI 53213
Email: info@halleonard.com

In Europe, contact:
Hal Leonard Europe Limited
42 Wigmore Street
Marylebone, London, W1U 2RN
Email: info@halleonardeurope.com

In Australia, contact:
Hal Leonard Australia Pty. Ltd.
4 Lentara Court
Cheltenham, Victoria, 3192 Australia
Email: info@halleonard.com.au

SPEECHLESS
from *Aladdin*

Music by Alan Menken
Lyrics by Benj Pasek and Justin Paul

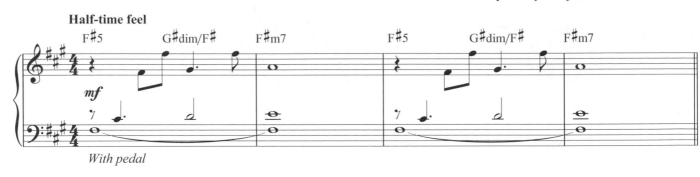

cry, and I won't start to crum - ble

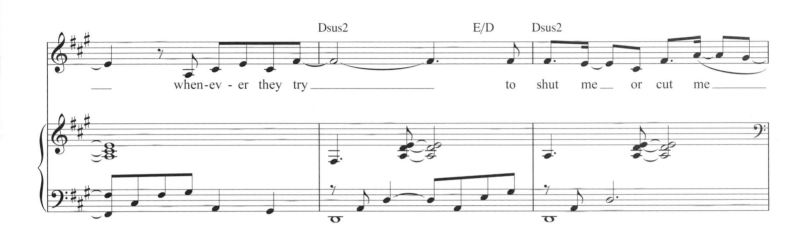

when-ev - er they try to shut me or cut me

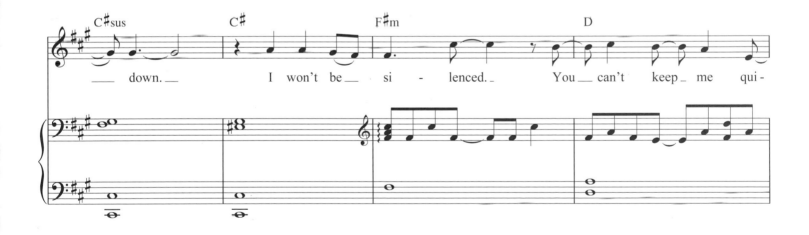

down. I won't be si - lenced. You can't keep me qui-

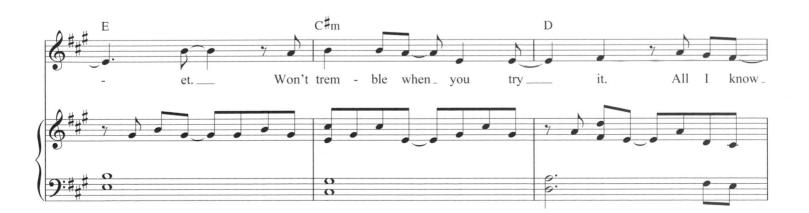

-et. Won't trem - ble when you try it. All I know

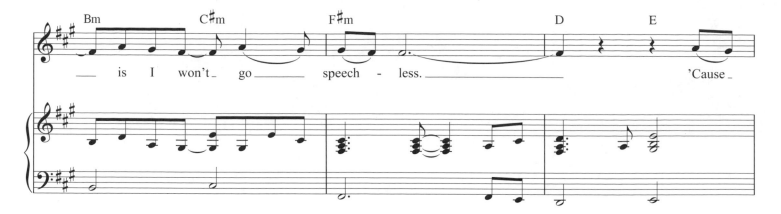

is I won't go ____ speech - less. _____ 'Cause _

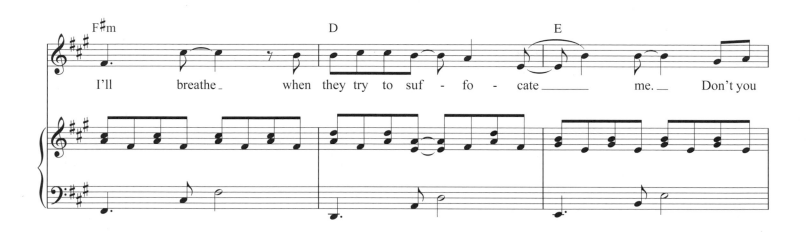

I'll breathe _ when they try to suf - fo - cate _____ me. _ Don't you

un - der - es - ti - mate _ me, 'cause I know _ that I won't go _____

speech - less. Writ - ten in stone, _ ev - 'ry

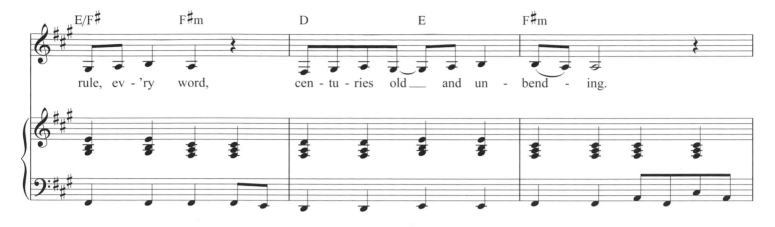

rule, ev-'ry word, cen-tu-ries old___ and un - bend - ing.

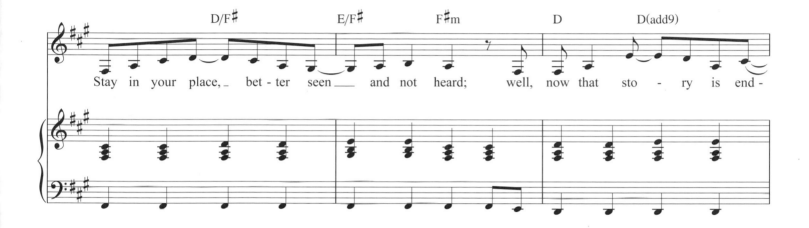

Stay in your place,___ bet-ter seen___ and not heard; well, now that sto - ry is end-

- ing. 'Cause I, I can-not start___ to crum - ble._____

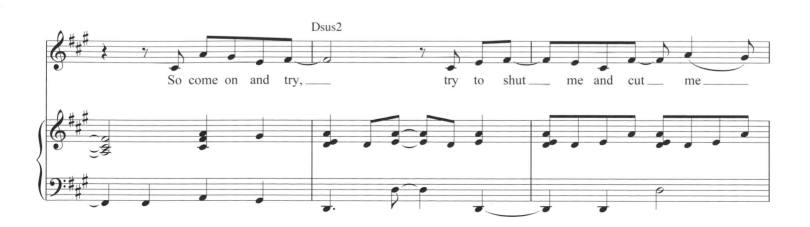

So come on and try,____ try to shut___ me and cut___ me

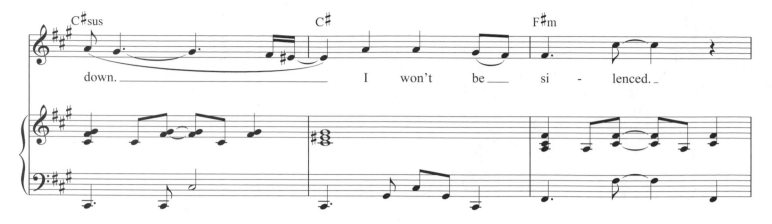

down. _____ I won't be __ si - lenced. __

You can't keep __ me qui - et. __ Won't trem - ble when __ you try __

__ it. All I know __ is I won't go _____ speech - less. Speech-

- less. __ Let the storm in. __ I can - not __ be bro -

- ken. No, I won't live un-spok - en, 'cause I know

that I won't go speech - less. Try to

lock me in this cage, I won't just lay me down and die. I will

take these brok - en wings, and watch me burn a - cross the sky.

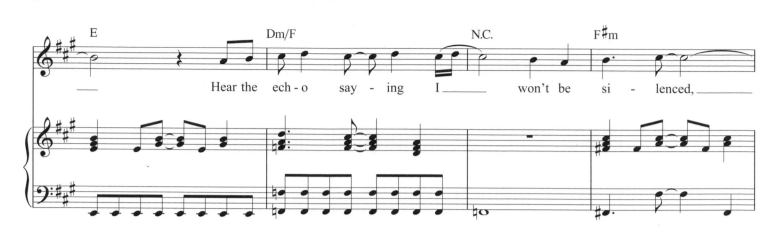

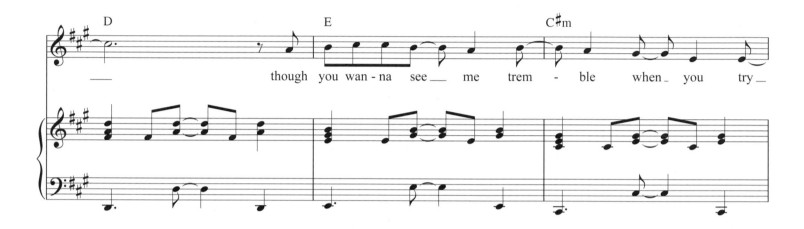

me. Don't you un-der-es-ti-mate me, 'cause I know

that I won't go speech-less. All I know is I won't go speech-

-less. Speech-less!

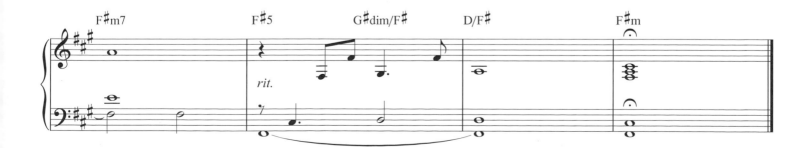

TOUCH THE SKY

from *Brave*

Music by Alexander L. Mandel
Lyrics by Alexander L. Mandel
and Mark Andrews

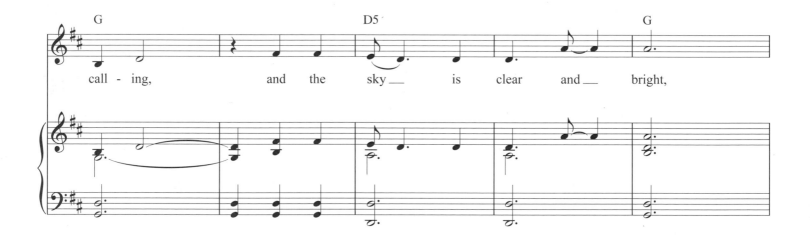

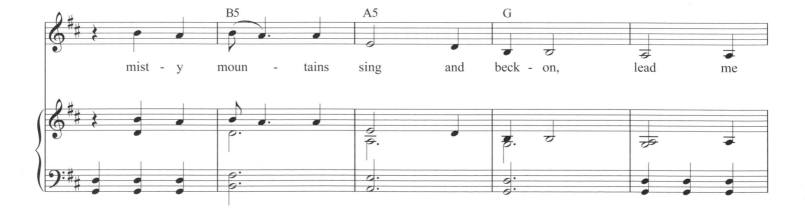

out in - to the light. I will ride,

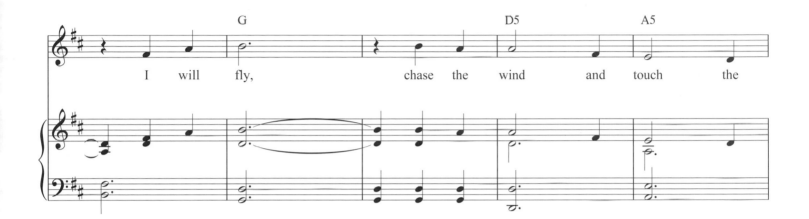

I will fly, chase the wind and touch the

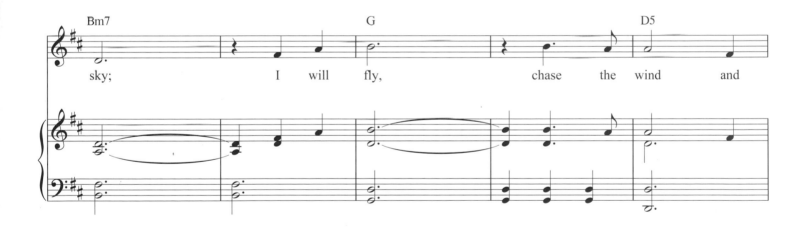

sky; I will fly, chase the wind and

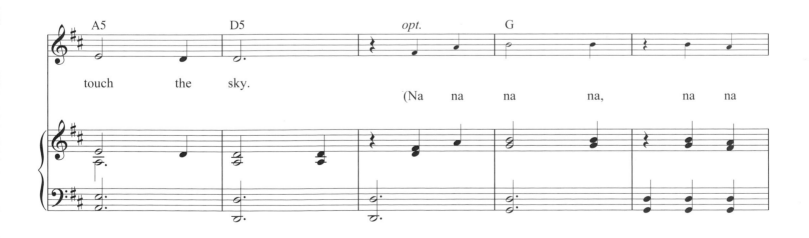

touch the sky. (Na na na na, na na

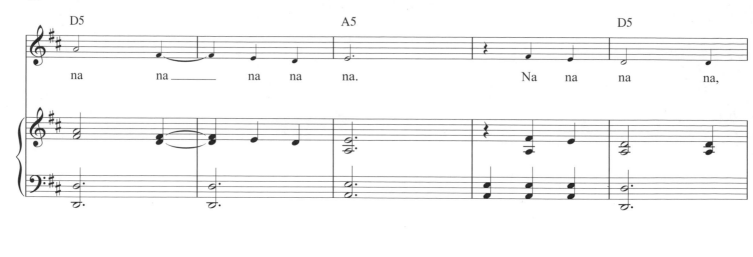

na   na ____ na   na   na.   Na   na   na   na,

na   na   na   na,   na   na   na   na ____ na   na

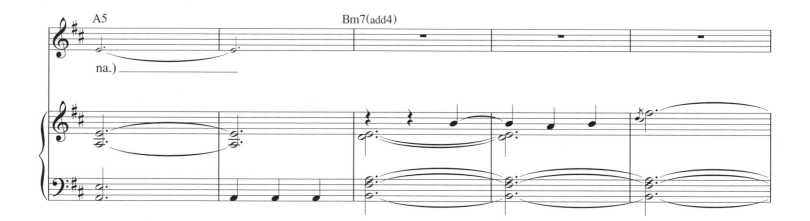

na.) ____

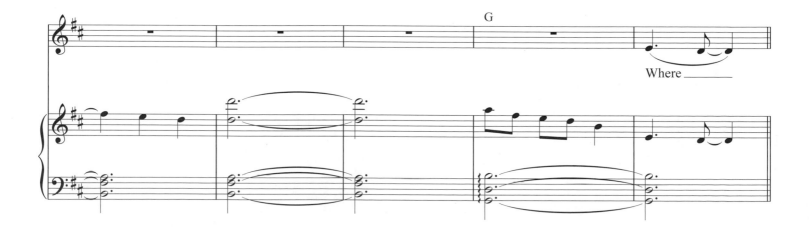

Where ____

CODA

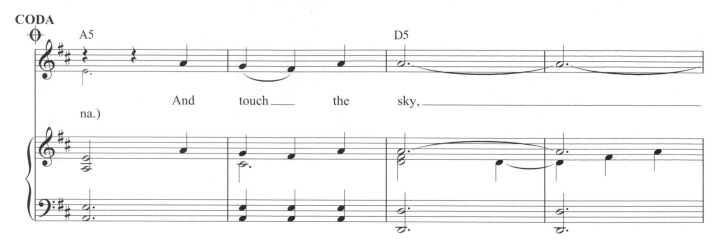

And touch ___ the sky, _____

na.)

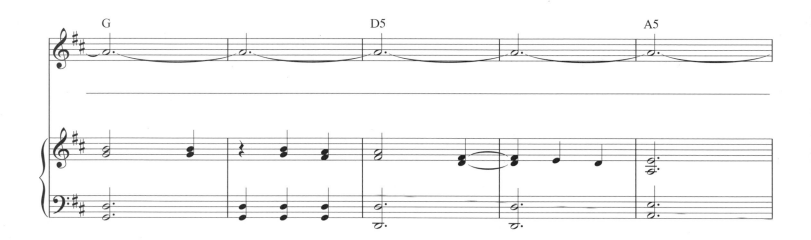

chase ___ the ___ wind, chase ___ the ___

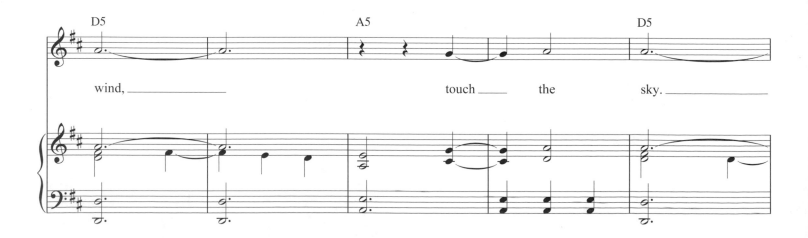

wind, _____ touch ___ the sky. _____

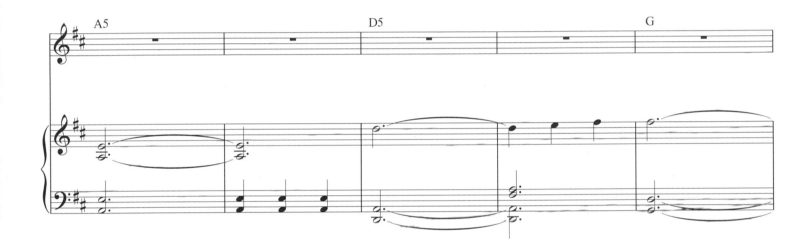

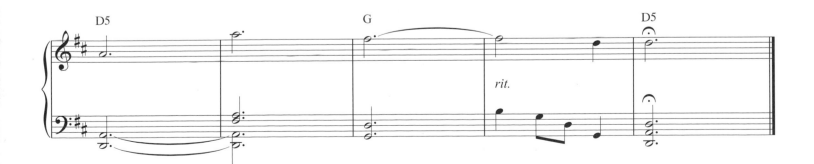

IF ONLY
from *Descendants*

Words and Music by Adam Anders,
Nikki Hassman and Par Astrom

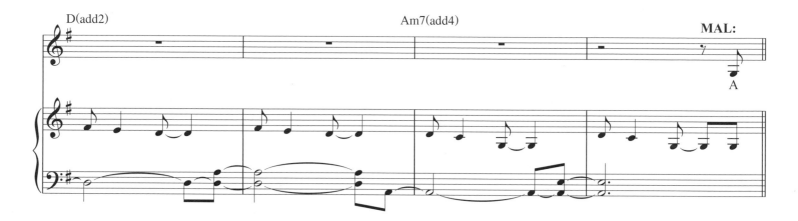

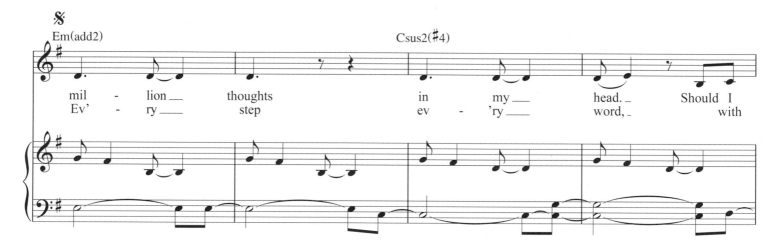

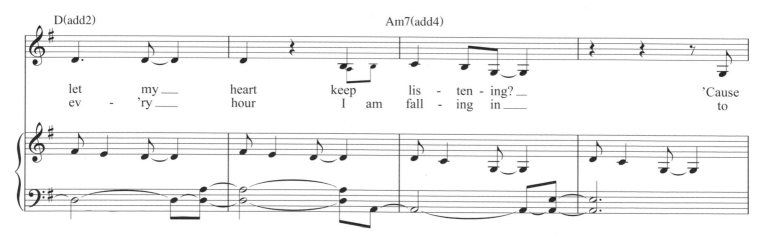

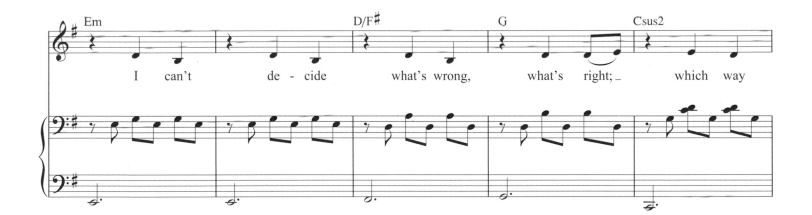

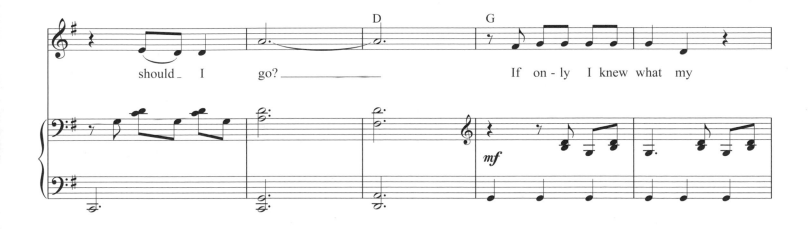

heart was tell - ing me. Don't know what I'm feel - ing;

is this __ just a __ dream? __ Ah oh, _____

yeah. If on - ly I could read the signs in __ front of me,

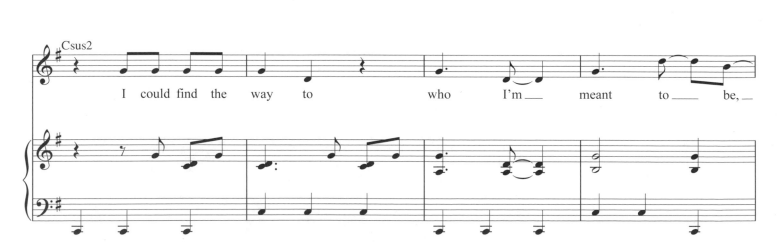

I could find the way to who I'm __ meant to __ be, __

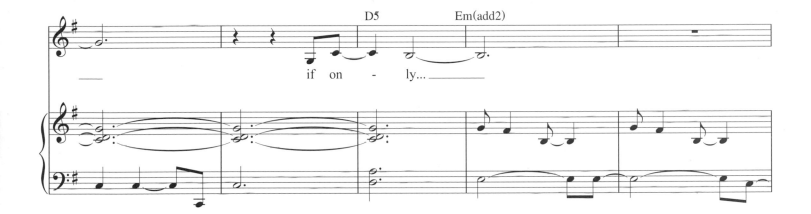

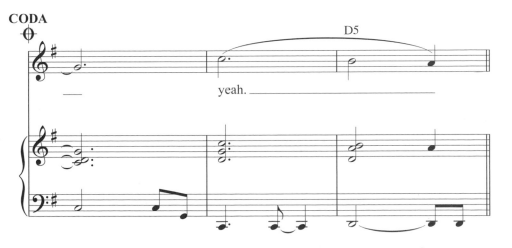

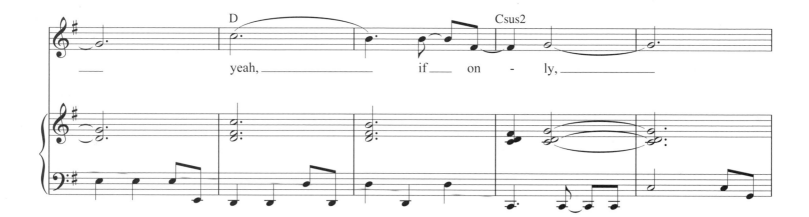

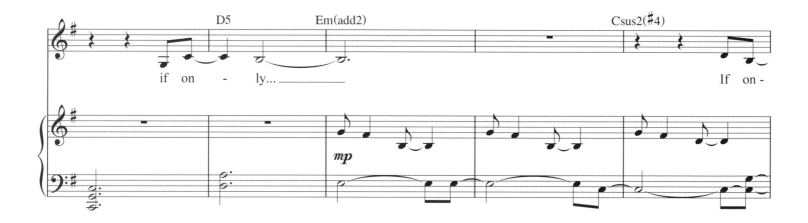

QUEEN OF MEAN

from *Descendants 3*

Written by Antonina Armato,
Tim James, Thomas Sturges
and Adam Schmalholz

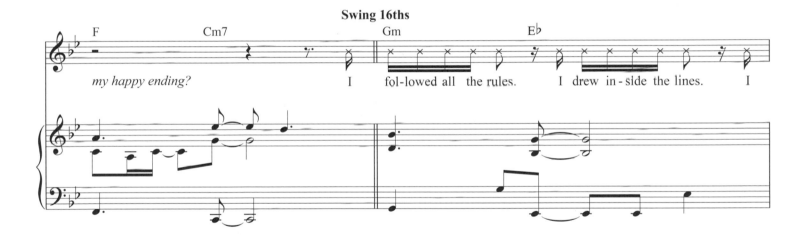

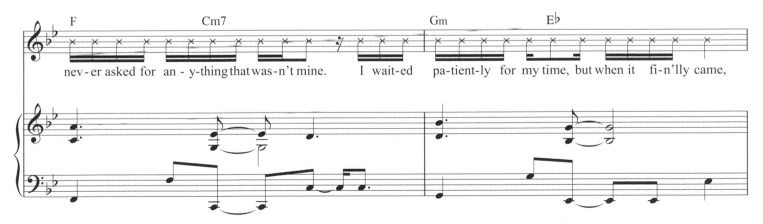

an-ger burns my skin, third de-gree. Now my blood's boil-ing hot-ter than a fier-y sea. There's no-

bod-y get-ting close to me. They're gon-na bow to the e-vil queen. Your night-mare's my dream. Just

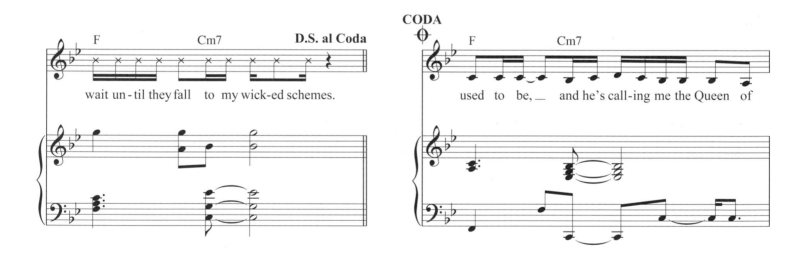

wait un-til they fall to my wick-ed schemes. **D.S. al Coda**

CODA

used to be, __ and he's call-ing me the Queen of

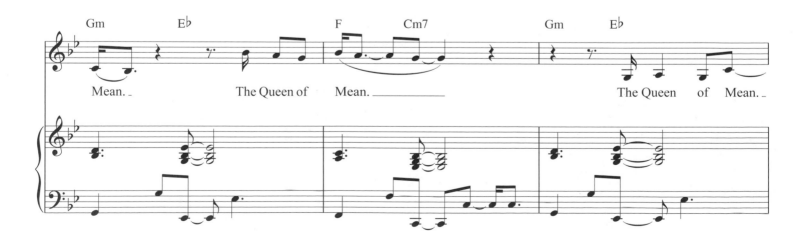

Mean. __ The Queen of Mean. _____ The Queen of Mean. _

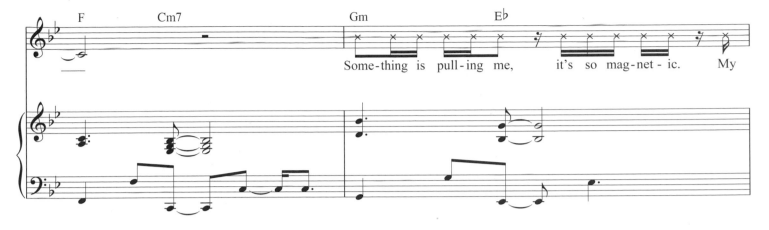

Some-thing is pull-ing me, it's so mag-net - ic. My

bod - y is mov - ing, un-sure where I'm head-ed. All of my sen-ses have left me de-fense-less. This

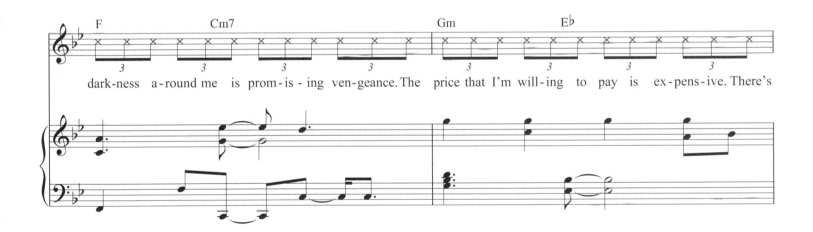

dark-ness a-round me is prom-is - ing ven-geance. The price that I'm will-ing to pay is ex-pens-ive. There's

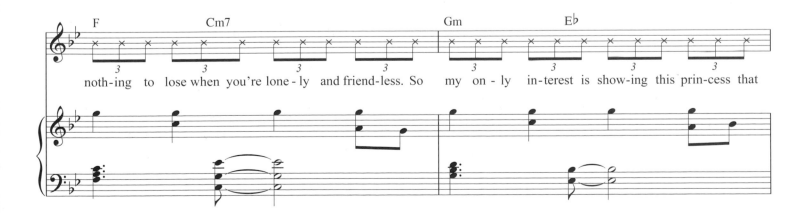

noth-ing to lose when you're lone - ly and friend-less. So my on - ly in-terest is show-ing this prin-cess that

FOR THE FIRST TIME IN FOREVER

from *Frozen*

Music and Lyrics by Kristen Anderson-Lopez
and Robert Lopez

With excitement

With pedal

mf

ANNA:

The win-dow is o - pen! So's _ that door! _ I

did-n't know they did that an - y - more. _ Who knew we owned _ eight thou - sand sal - ad

plates?

For years I've roamed _ these emp - ty halls. _

Why have a ball - room with no balls? Fi - nal - ly, they're o - p'ning up the

gates! There'll be ac - tual real live peo - ple;

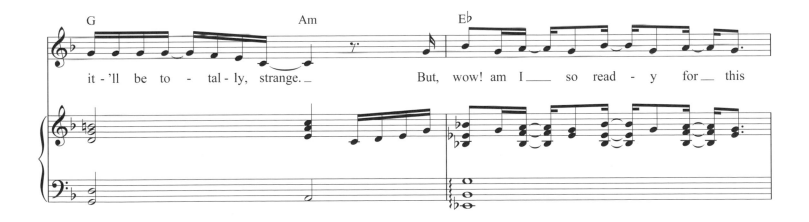

it - 'll be to - tal - ly, strange. But, wow! am I so read - y for this

Expressively

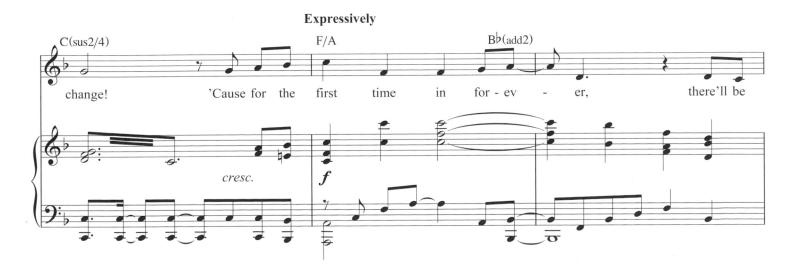

change! 'Cause for the first time in for - ev - er, there'll be

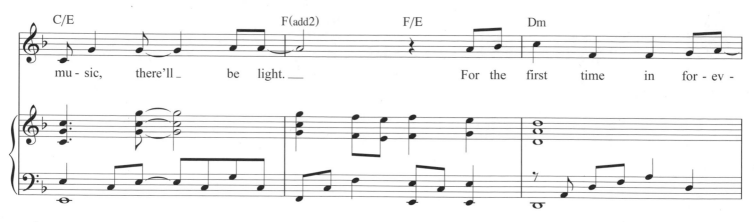

mu - sic, there'll _ be light. __ For the first time in for - ev -

- er, I'll be danc - ing through_ the night. __ Don't

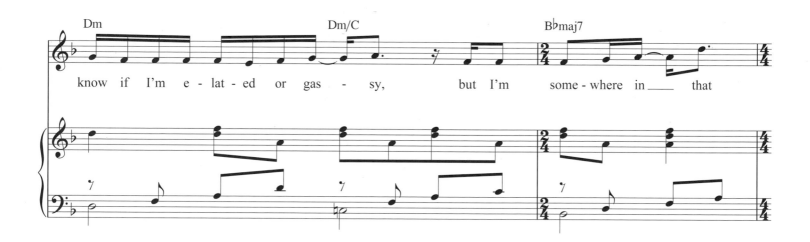

know if I'm e - lat - ed or gas - sy, but I'm some - where in ____ that

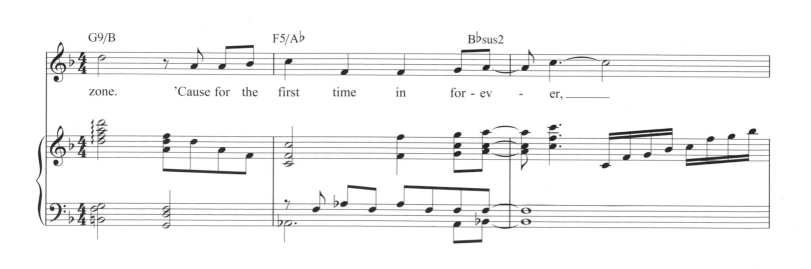

zone. 'Cause for the first time in for - ev - er, _____

beau-ti-ful stran - ger, tall _ and fair. _ I wan - na stuff _ some choc - 'late in _ my

face! But then we laugh and talk _ all eve - ning, which is

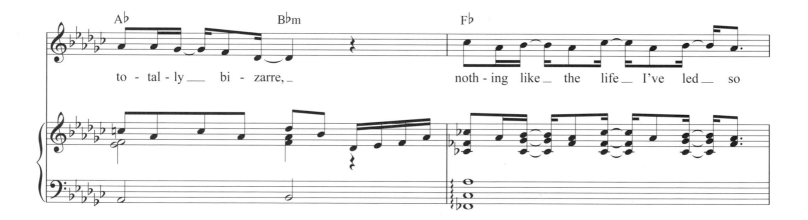

to - tal - ly _ bi - zarre, _ noth-ing like _ the life _ I've led _ so

far. For the first time in for - ev -

-er, there'll be mag-ic, there'll _ be fun. _ For the

first time in for-ev - er, I could be no-ticed by _ some-one. _

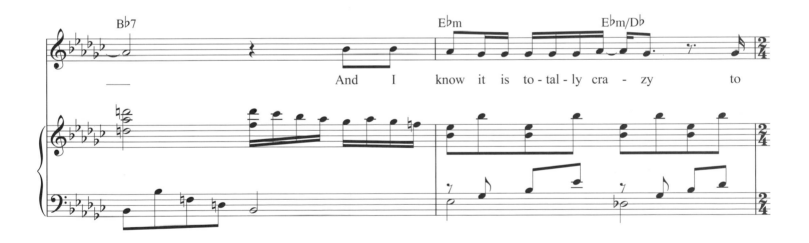

And I know it is to-tal-ly cra - zy to

dream I'd find _ ro - mance, but for the first time in for-ev -

er, ___

at least_ I've got_ a chance._

___

For the first time in for - ev -

- er, I'm get-ting what I'm dream - ing of: ___ a

chance to change_ my lone - ly world, a chance to find_ true love._

I know it all ends to-mor-row,____ so it

has to be____ to-day. 'Cause for the first time in for-ev-

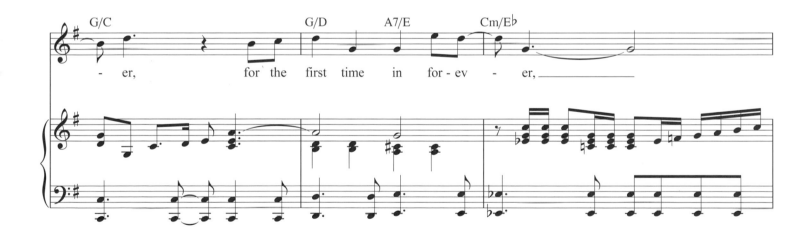

-er, for the first time in for-ev - er,_____

noth-ing's in my____ way!_____

LET IT GO
from *Frozen: The Broadway Musical*

Music and Lyrics by Kristen Anderson-Lopez
and Robert Lopez

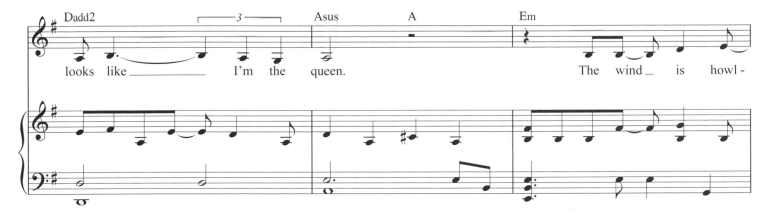

looks like _____ I'm the queen. The wind __ is howl -

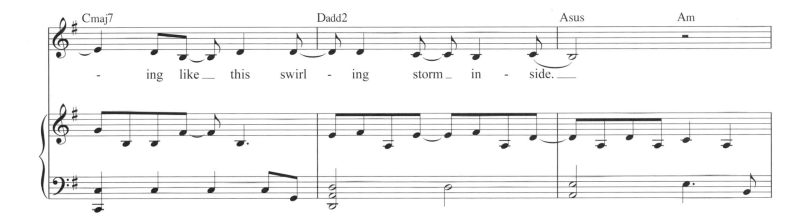

- ing like __ this swirl - ing storm __ in - side. __

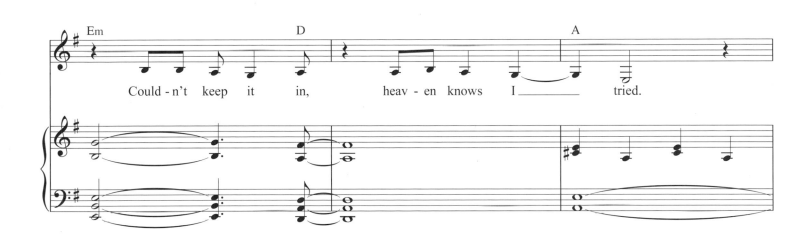

Could -n't keep it in, heav - en knows I _____ tried.

Don't let ___ them in, _____ don't let ___ them see.

Be the good girl you al-ways have_ to be. Con-ceal._ Don't feel._

_ Don't let_ them know._____ Well, now_

_ they know._____ Let it go,___ let it go._

Can't hold it back an-y-more._ Let it go,_

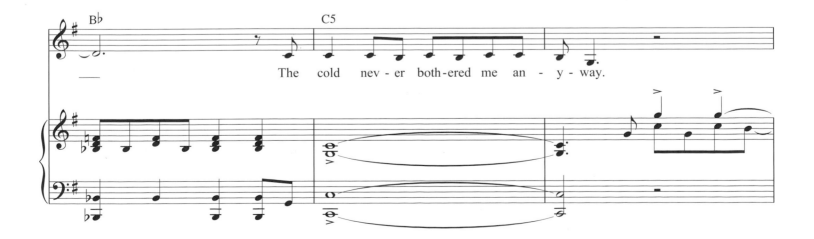

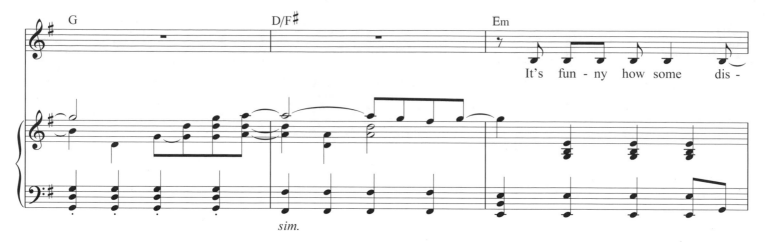

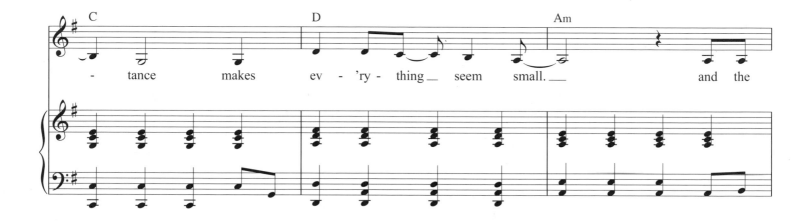

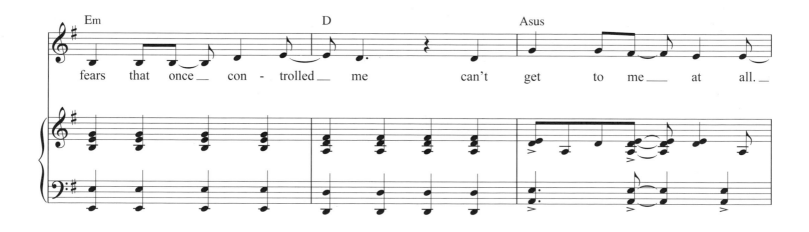

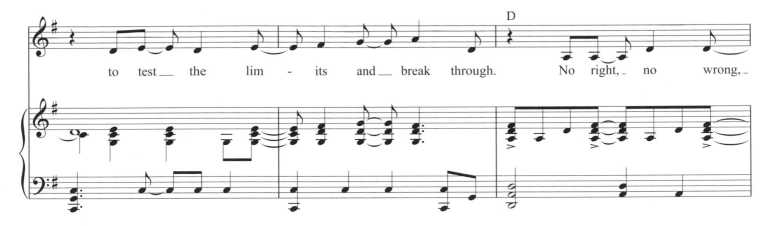

You'll nev - er see __ me cry. __

Here __ I __ stand, __ and here __ I'll __ stay. __ Let the

storm rage __ on. __

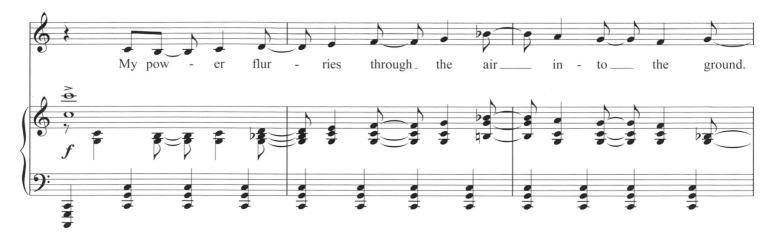

My pow - er flur - ries through the air in - to the ground.

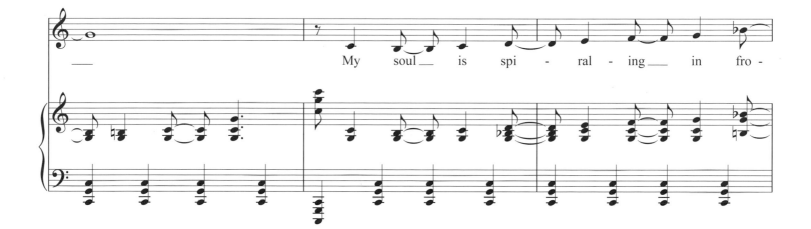

My soul is spi - ral - ing in fro -

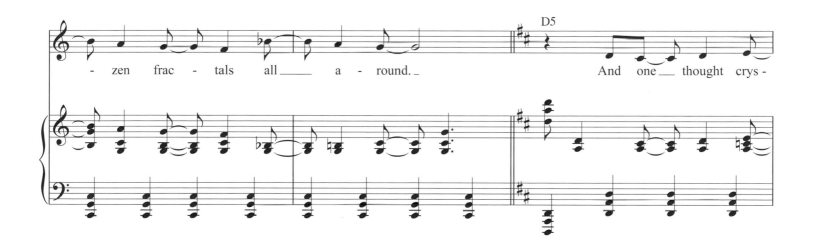

- zen frac - tals all a - round. And one thought crys -

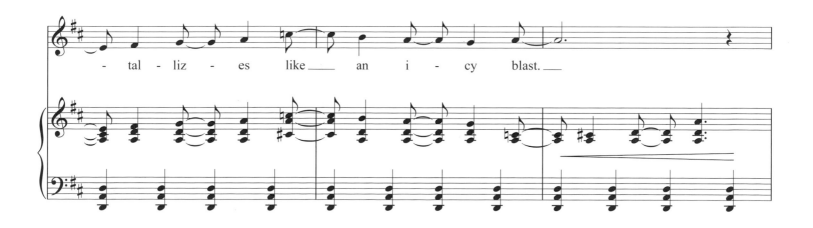

- tal - liz - es like an i - cy blast.

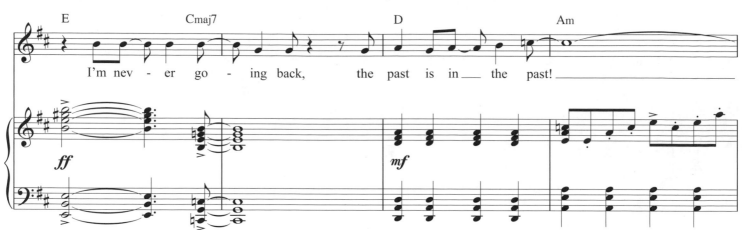

I'm nev - er go - ing back, the past is in ___ the past! _____

___ Let it go! ___ Let it go! ___ And I'll rise ___

___ like the break ___ of dawn _____ Let it go! ___ Let it go! ___

That per - fect girl ___ is ___ gone. ___

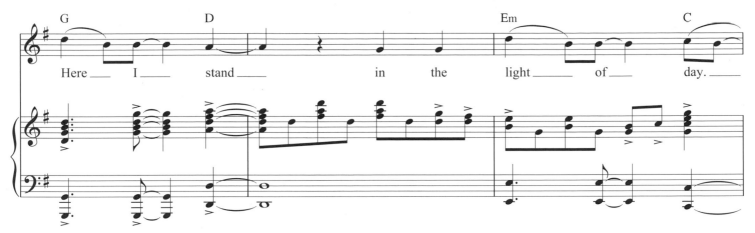

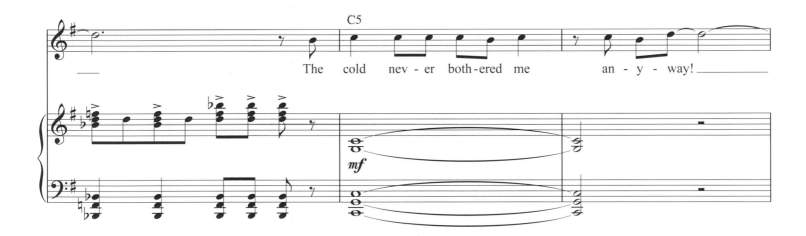

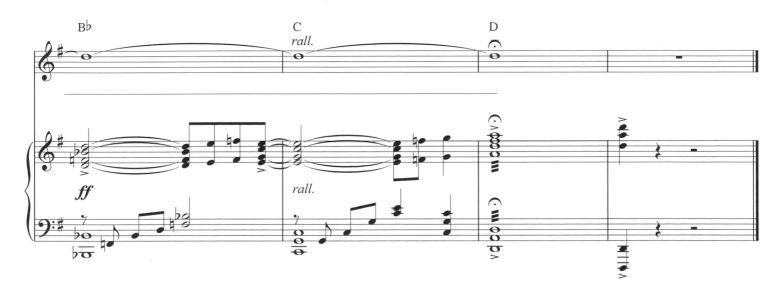

INTO THE UNKNOWN

from *Frozen 2*

Music and Lyrics by Kristen Anderson-Lopez
and Robert Lopez

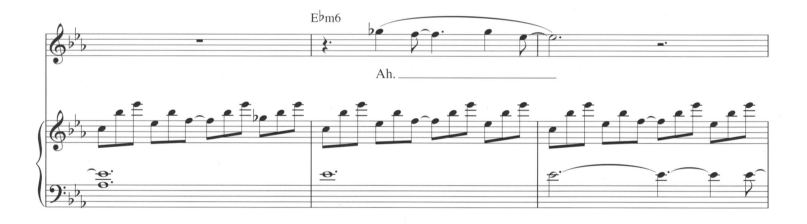

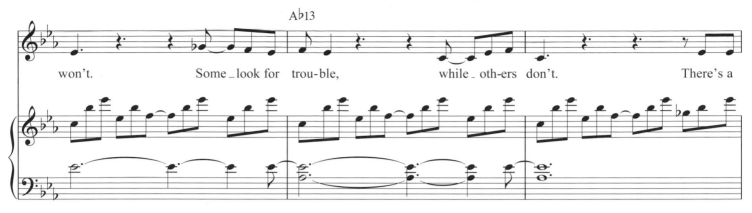

won't.   Some _ look for trou-ble,   while _ oth-ers don't.   There's a

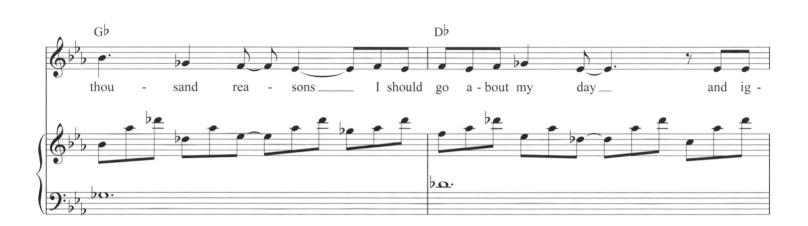

thou - sand   rea - sons _____ I should go a-bout my   day _____   and ig-

nore   your whis - pers, _____ which I   wish   would go a - way... _____ Oh. _____

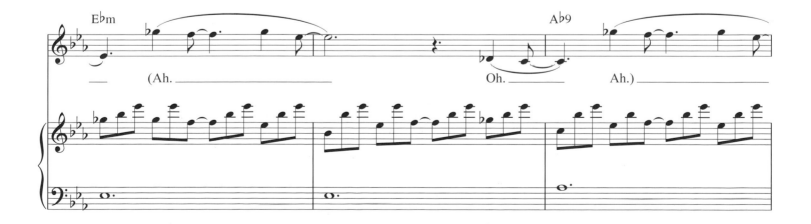

_____   (Ah. _____   Oh. _____   Ah.) _____

With determination

You're not a voice, you're just a ring-ing in my ear, __ and __ if I

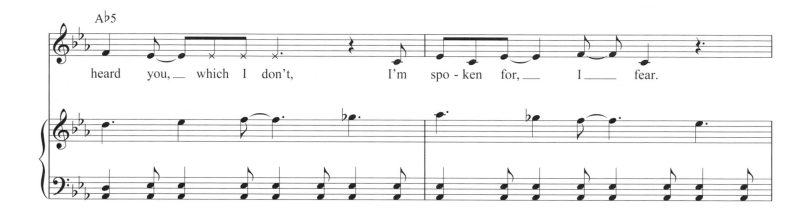

heard you, __ which I don't, I'm spo-ken for, __ I ____ fear.

Ev - 'ry-one I've ev - er loved is here with - in these walls. __ I'm

sor - ry, se - cret si - ren, but I'm block-ing out your calls. __ I've

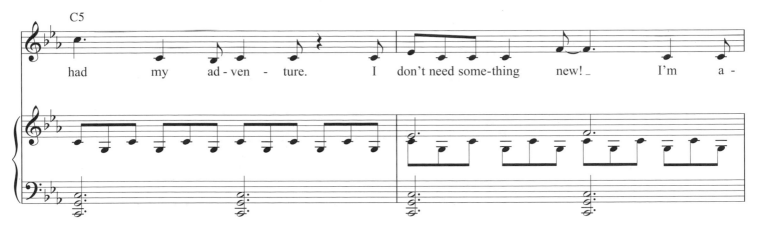

had my ad-ven-ture. I don't need some-thing new! I'm a-

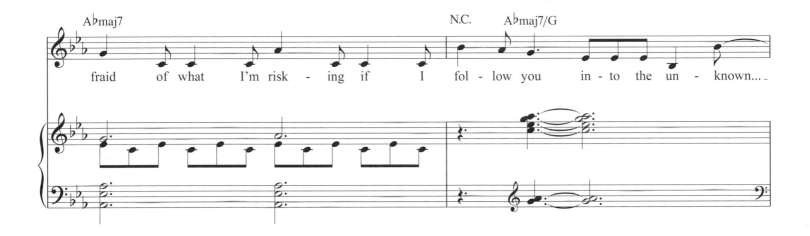

fraid of what I'm risk-ing if I fol-low you in-to the un-known....

in-to the un - known...

in-to the un - known...

in-to the un - known!

What do you want? 'Cause you've been keep-ing me a - wake. Are you

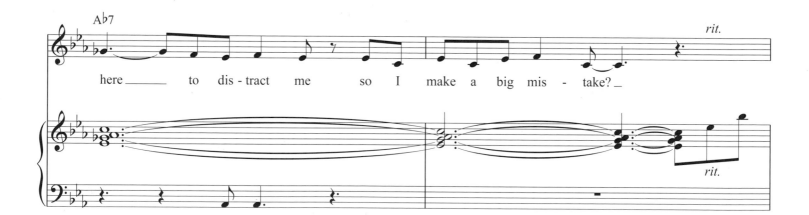

here to dis - tract me so I make a big mis - take?

Slower, with freedom

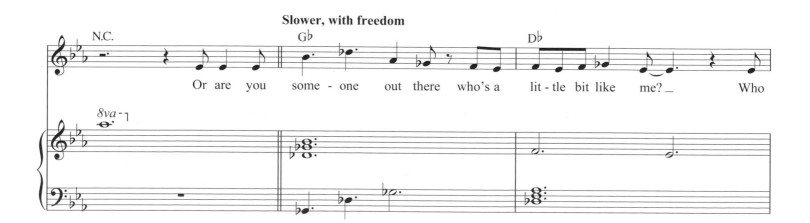

Or are you some - one out there who's a lit - tle bit like me? Who

knows   deep   down   I'm not   where   I'm meant to   be? __   Ev -'ry

Driving

day's   a   lit - tle   hard - er   as   I   feel   my   pow - er   grow! _

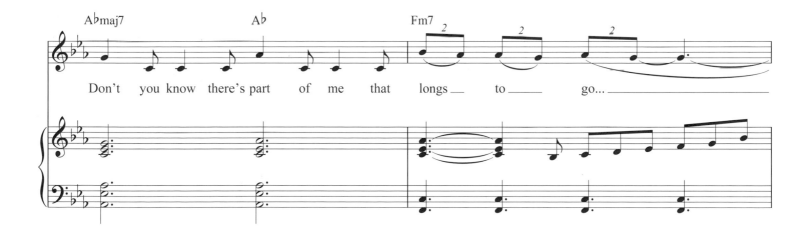

Don't   you   know   there's part   of   me   that   longs __   to ____   go... _____

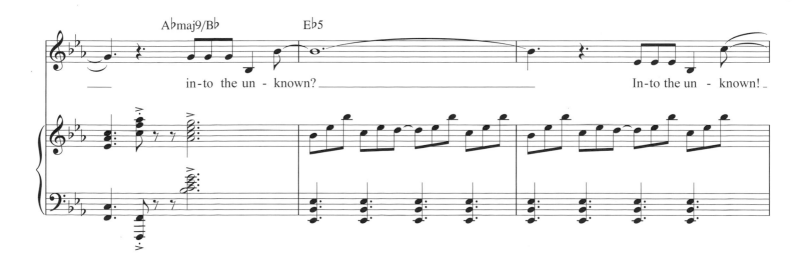

___   in-to   the un - known? _____   In-to   the un - known! _

In-to the un - known!

(Ah. Ah.) Oh, are you

out there? Do you know me? Can you feel me? Can you show me? Ah,

(Ah, ah, ah,

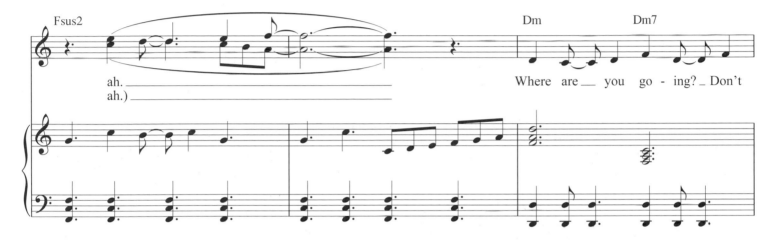

ah,   ah,   ah,
ah,   ah,   ah,

ah.   Where are _ you go - ing? _ Don't
ah.)

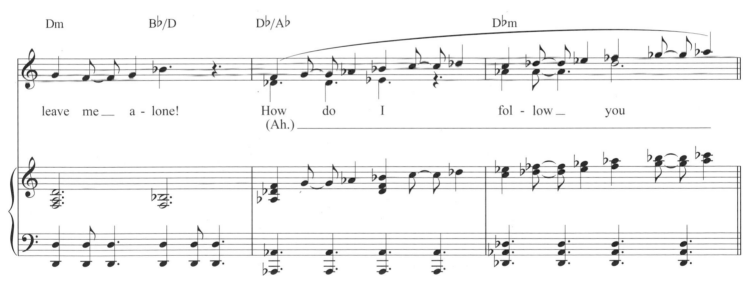

leave me _ a - lone!   How do I fol - low _ you
(Ah.)

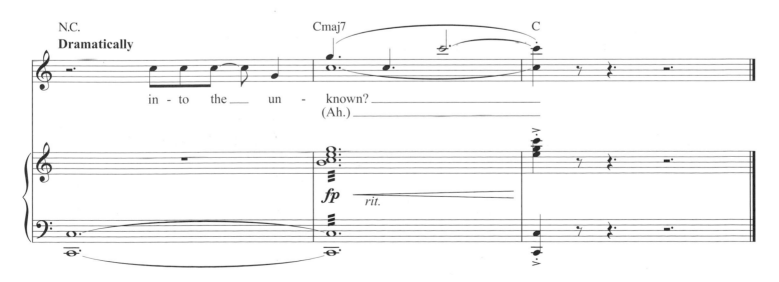

Dramatically

in - to the _ un - known?
(Ah.)

TRUE LOVE

from *Frozen: The Broadway Musical*

Music and Lyrics by Kristen Anderson-Lopez
and Robert Lopez

ANNA:
I've sat a-lone in this room be-fore, hours and hours on end. I know this de-lu-sion-al wish the door would o-pen to re-veal a friend. I know this sol-i-tude, I know this kind of cold, but I had faith in what the

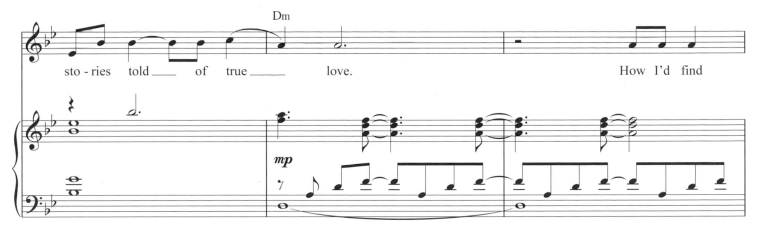

sto - ries told ___ of true ___ love. How I'd find

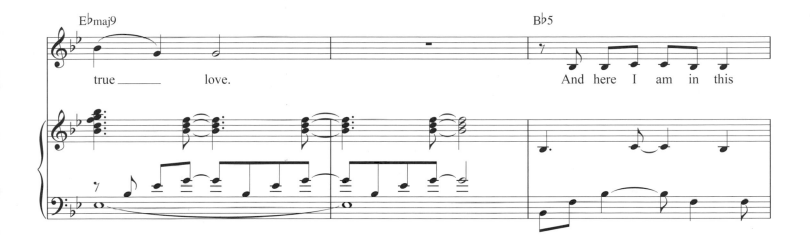

true ___ love. And here I am in this

room a - gain, ___ just as lost and small. ___ That

lone - ly girl ___ with a des - p'rate heart ___ is who I am, ___

af - ter all. ___ There's no es - cap - ing her, but now the dream is gone

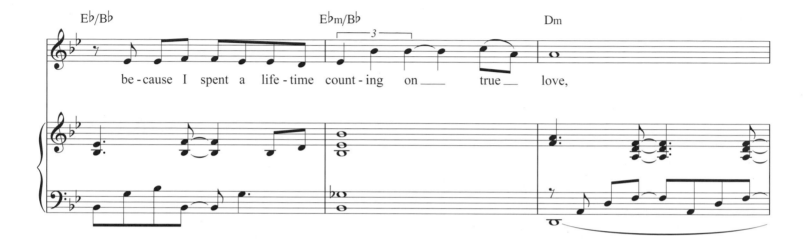

be - cause I spent a life - time count - ing on ___ true ___ love,

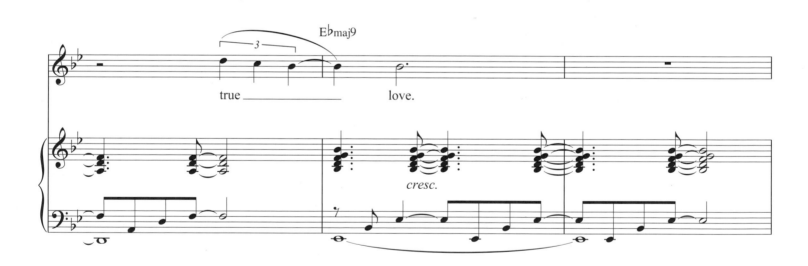

true ___ love.

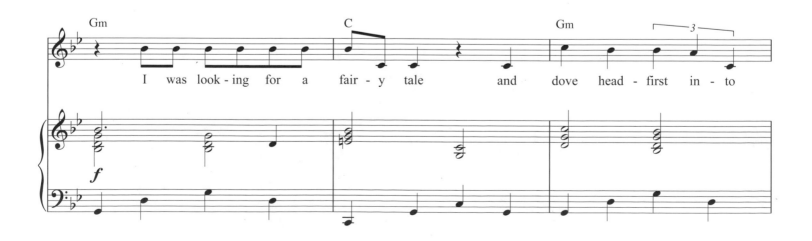

I was look - ing for a fair - y tale and dove head - first in - to

in the plan.___ Dream-ing got me here, and yet the dream won't die. I

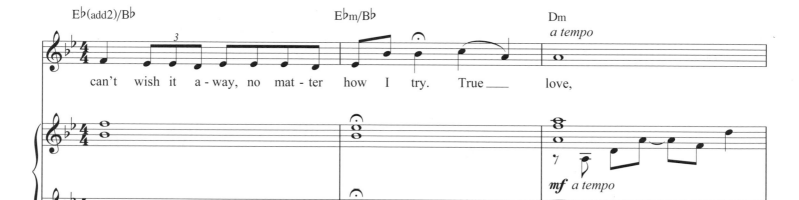

can't wish it a-way, no mat-ter how I try. True___ love,

true _____ love, true _____ love. ___

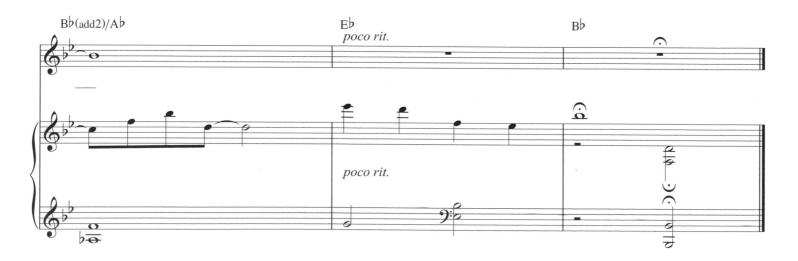

THE PLACE WHERE LOST THINGS GO

from *Mary Poppins Returns*

Music by Marc Shaiman
Lyrics by Scott Wittman and Marc Shaiman

Wond-'ring where to find what you tru - ly miss. May-be all those things that

you love so are wait-ing in the place where the lost things go.

Mem - o - ries you've shared, gone for good you feared. They're all a-round you still, though they've

dis - ap-peared. Noth-ing's real - ly left or lost with-out a trace.

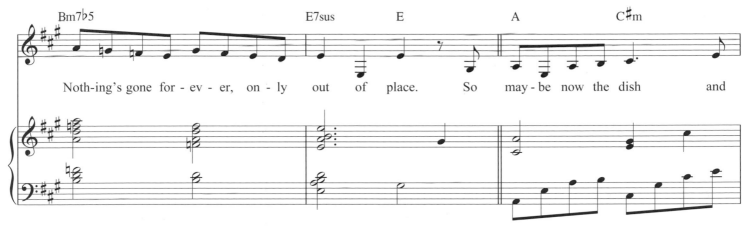

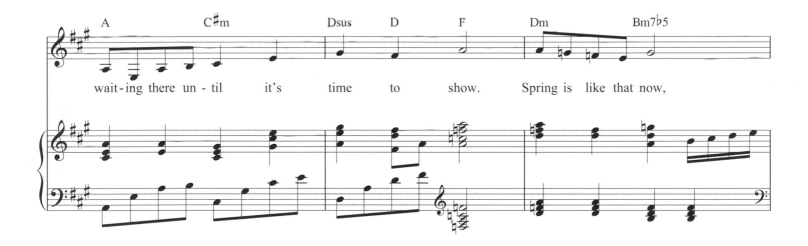

WATCH WHAT HAPPENS

from *Newsies The Musical*

Music by Alan Menken
Lyrics by Jack Feldman

Ha, it's a cinch; it can prac-ti-c'ly write it-self. And let's pray it does, 'cause as
fact is he's al-so the face of the strike. What a face! Face the fact. That's a

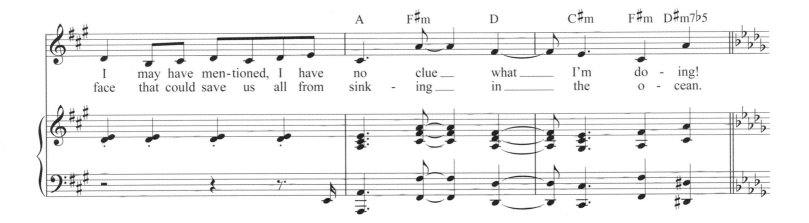

I may have men-tioned, I have no clue___ what___ I'm do-ing!
face that could save us all from sink - ing___ in___ the o - cean.

Am I in-sane? This is what I've been wait-ing for! Well, that, plus the scream-ing of
Like some one said, "Pow - er tends to cor-rupt and ab-so - lute pow-er..." Wait! Wait!"...Cor-

half cra-zy ed - i - tors: "A girl?" "It's a girl?! How the hell..." "Is that e - ven le - gal?"
rupts ab - so - lute-ly." That is gen - ius but give me some time, I'll be twice as good as

"Look, just go and get her!" Not on-ly that there's the
that six months from... nev-er. Just look a-round at the

sto-ry be-hind the sto-ry: thou-sands of chil-dren ex-ploit-ed, in-vis-i-ble. Speak
world we're in-her-it-ing and think of the one we'll cre-ate. Their mis-take is they got

up, take a stand, and there's some-one to write a-bout it. That's how things
old. That is not a mis-take we'll be mak-ing. No, sir, we'll stay young

get bet-ter. Give life's lit-tle guys some
for-ev-er! Give those kids and me the

ink, and ___ when ___ it dries, just watch what ___ hap -
brand - new ___ cen - tu - ry and watch what ___ hap -

- pens! ___ Those kids will live and breathe right ___ on ___
- pens! ___ It's Da - vid and Go - li - ath, ___ do ___

___ the page and once they're ___ cen - ter stage you
___ or die! The fight is ___ on, _____ and I can't

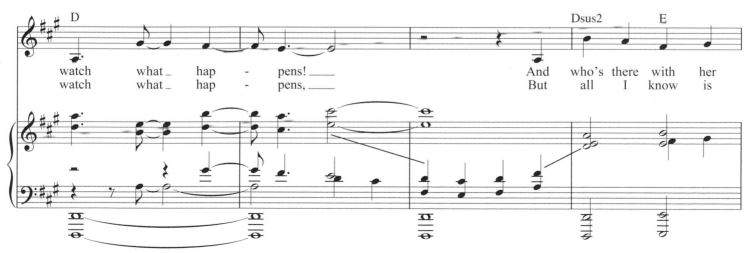

watch what ___ hap - pens! ___ And who's there with her
watch what ___ hap - pens, ___ But all I know is

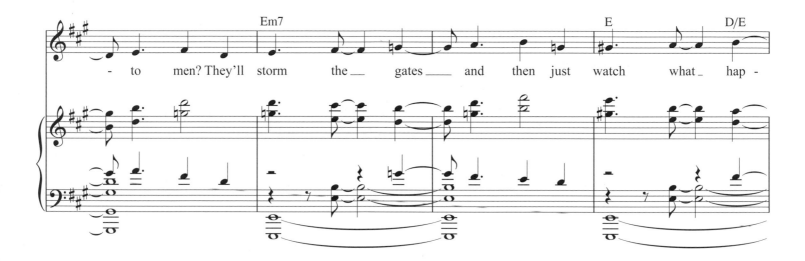

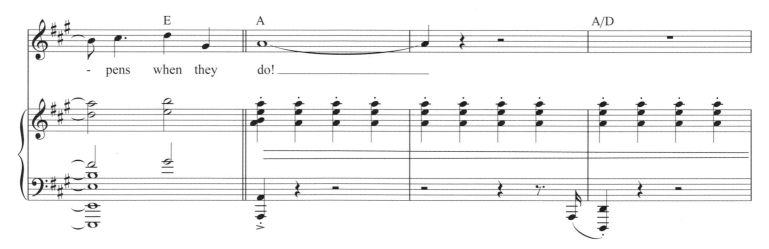

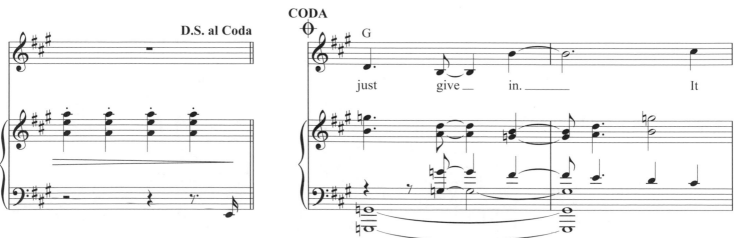

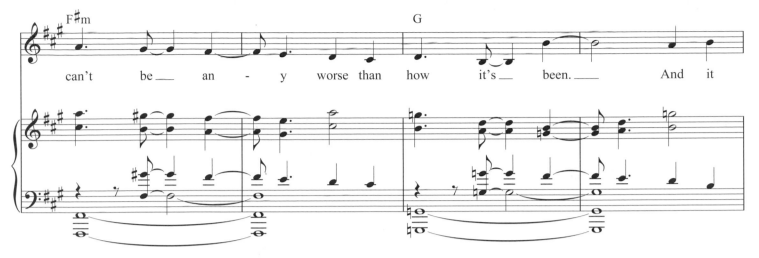

can't be __ an - y worse than how it's __ been. __ And it

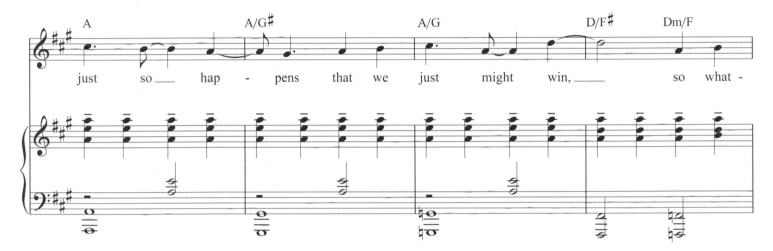

just so __ hap - pens that we just might win, __ so what -

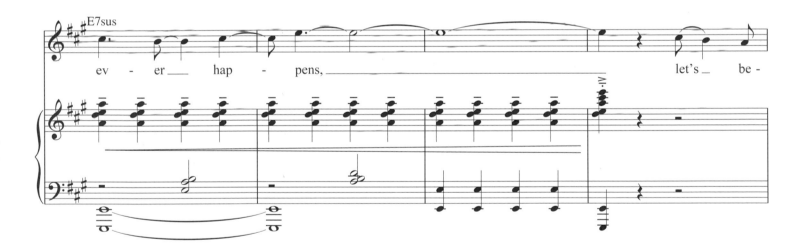

ev - er __ hap - pens, _____ let's __ be -

gin! _____

WHEN WILL MY LIFE BEGIN?

from *Tangled*

Music by Alan Menken
Lyrics by Glenn Slater

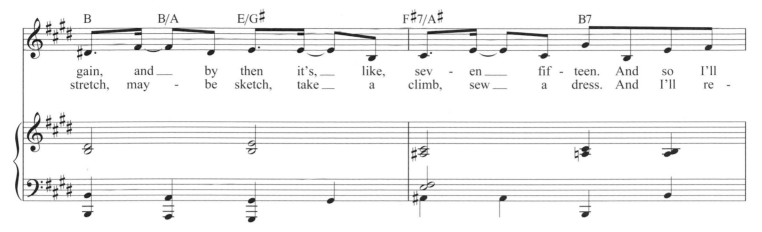

gain, and ___ by then it's, ___ like, sev - en ___ fif - teen. And so I'll
stretch, may - be sketch, take ___ a climb, sew ___ a dress. And I'll re -

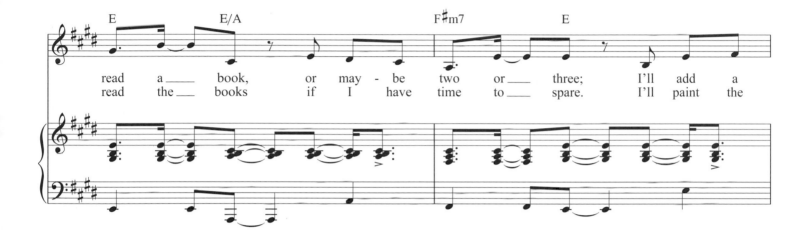

read a ___ book, or may - be two or ___ three; I'll add a
read the ___ books if I have time to ___ spare. I'll paint the

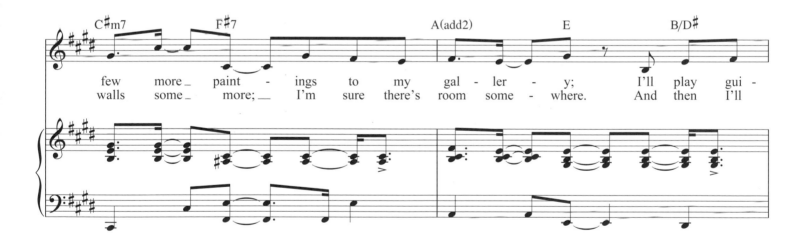

few more ___ paint - ings to my gal - ler - y; I'll play gui -
walls some ___ more; ___ I'm sure there's room some - where. And then I'll

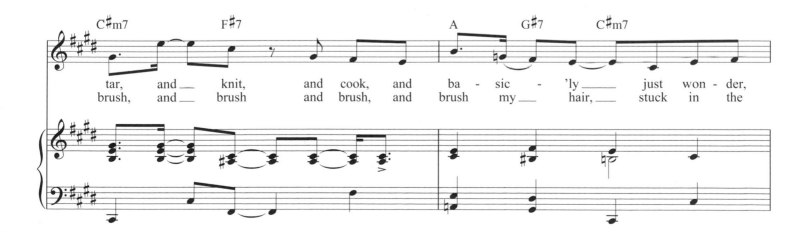

tar, and ___ knit, and cook, and ba - sic - 'ly ___ just won - der,
brush, and ___ brush and brush, and brush my ___ hair, ___ stuck in the

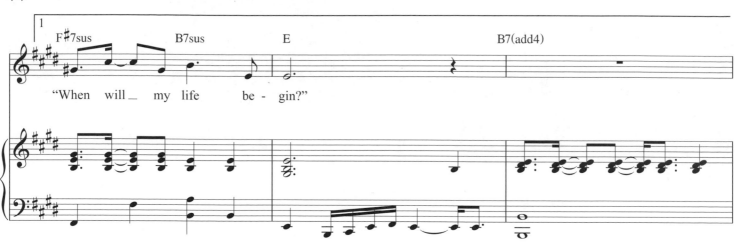

"When will my life be - gin?"

same place I've al - ways been, and I'll keep won - d'ring and won - d'ring and

won - d'ring and won - d'ring, "When will my life be - gin?"

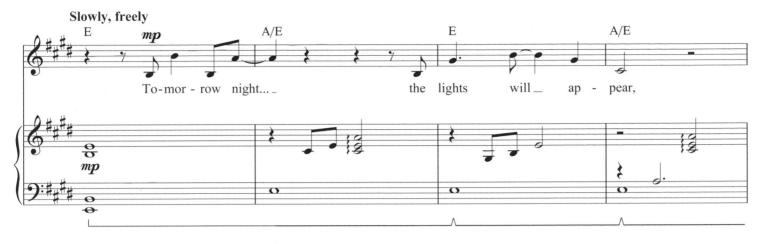

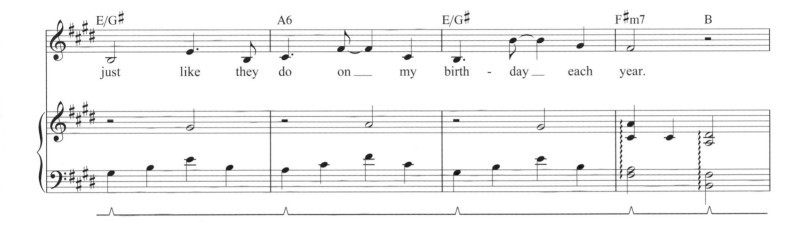

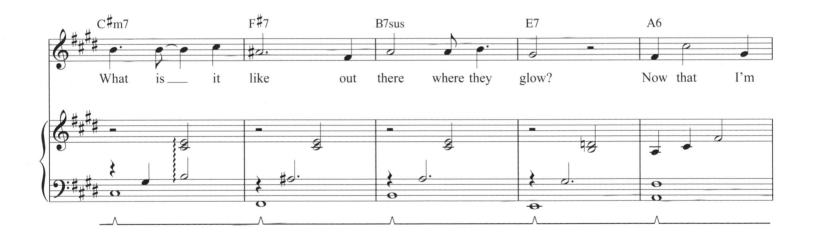

HOW FAR I'LL GO
from *Moana*

Music and Lyrics by
Lin-Manuel Miranda

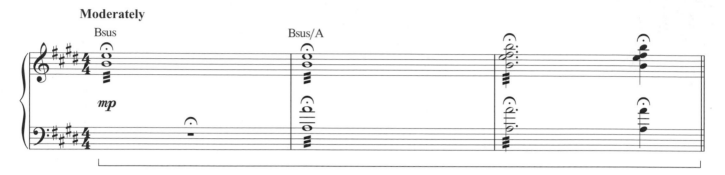

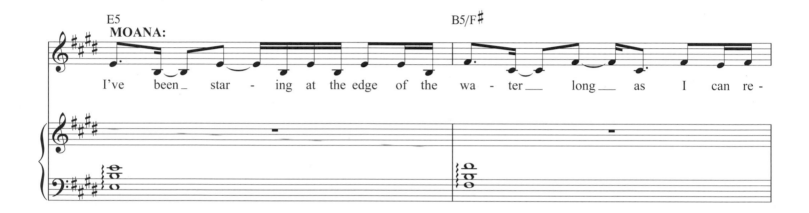

I've been _ star - ing at the edge of the wa - ter _ long _ as I can re -

mem - ber, _ nev - er real-ly know-ing why. I wish I could be the per - fect

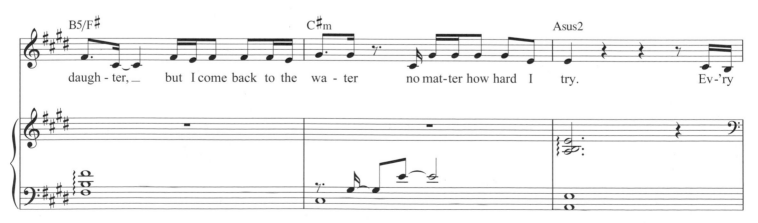

daugh - ter, _ but I come back to the wa - ter no mat-ter how hard I try. Ev-'ry

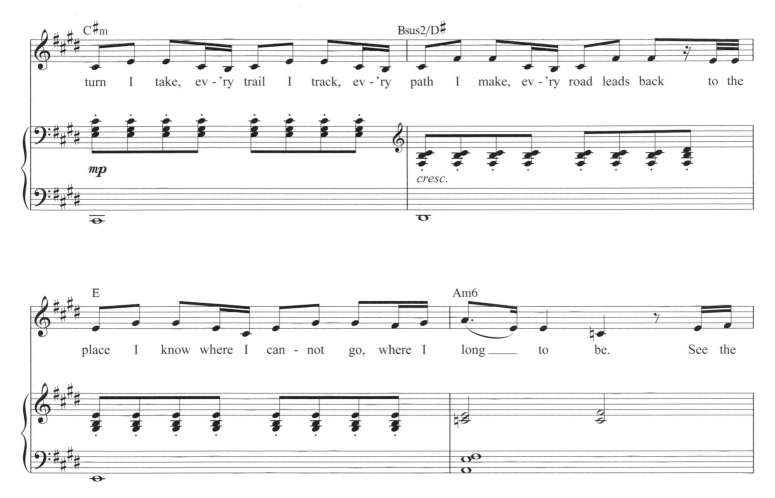

turn I take, ev-'ry trail I track, ev-'ry path I make, ev-'ry road leads back to the

place I know where I can-not go, where I long ___ to be. See the

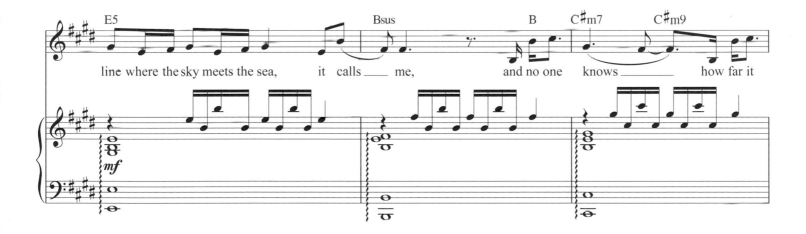

line where the sky meets the sea, it calls ___ me, and no one knows ___ how far it

goes. ___ If the wind in my sail on the sea stays be-hind ___ me, one day I'll

know. _____ If I go, there's just no tell-ing how far I'll go. I __ know _ ev-'ry-bod-y on this

is - land _ seems _ so hap-py on this is - land. _ Ev -'ry-thing is by de - sign. _

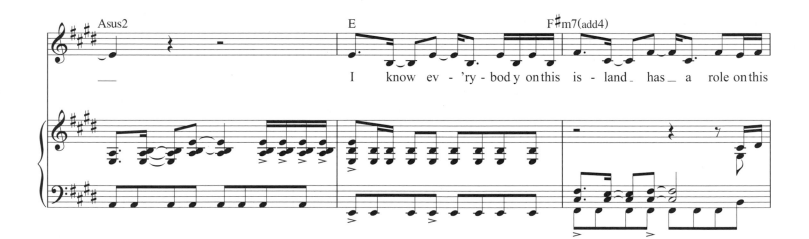

__ I know ev -'ry - bod y on this is - land _ has _ a role on this

is - land, _ so may-be I can roll with mine. _ I can

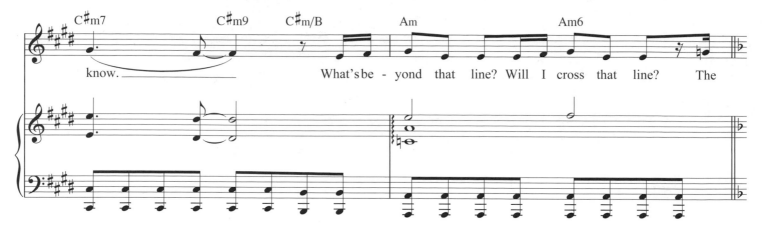

know._____ What's be - yond that line? Will I cross that line? The

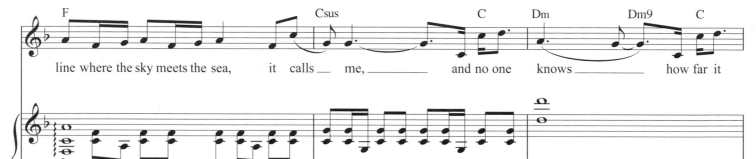

line where the sky meets the sea, it calls __ me, _____ and no one knows _____ how far it

goes. _____ If the wind in my sail on the sea stays be - hind __ me, one day I'll

know _____ how far I'll go! _____